Quilted Travel Bags

Designs by Jerry Shaw

HOUSE of WHITE BIRCHES
PUBLISHERS SINCE 1947

Make a Coordinated Set of Travel Bags

Today's quilters are on the go and always need just the right-size bag in which to carry everything necessary for a trip. This book has instructions for bags in a variety of sizes to fit the bill. Whether you desire a large open bag to hold clothes for a weekend, an overnight bag for a quick trip or just a small purse with compartments, you will find the perfect-size bag for your needs.

Today's large selection of upholstery or heavyweight fabrics makes it possible to make a set of bags to match any personality. Choose fabrics that are designed to take a beating and won't show dirt or wear and tear to make your set last for many years to come.

Table of Contents

Air Travel Bag 8

Companion Purse 16

Barrel Bag 22

Extender Tote 26

Handy Wallet 32

Mini Pocket Purse 39

The Weekender 43

HOUSE OF WHITE BIRCHES, BERNE, INDIANA 46711 DRGNETWORK.COM

General Instructions

There are some general instructions that apply to the stitching of all bags in this book. Individual instructions are given for each bag but if you want to make an entire matching set of bags, the list of materials needed and cutting diagrams are given here as well.

Basic Instructions

• All seam allowances are ⅜" unless otherwise noted. The seam allowances are included in the cut sizes for each project.

• Use an average stitch length of 10–12 stitches per inch or 2.5 or 3mm for all sewing unless otherwise instructed.

• Square one end of fabric and cut off selvage edges before beginning to cut pieces.

• A serger is helpful for finishing all seams after stitching. It reduces bulk and allows a seam to lie flat.

• Quilted fabric with a lengthwise-grain pattern requires precise cutting to guarantee straight lines on the finished project.

• Cut all bag pieces from a single thickness of fabric.

• Label each piece after cutting.

• Any piece label that includes IP indicates that it will be used for an inside pocket; an L indicates a lining piece.

• The length of fabric needed is often determined by the desired length of the straps.

• The brown-and-tan stripe used in the sample is cut on the crosswise grain of the fabric. Close attention must be paid to the pattern layout to match the stripes at the tops and bottoms of the bags as well as matching the stripes on the pockets.

• To form zipper pulls, cut 6" pieces of ⅜"-wide grosgrain ribbon, cutting each end on a diagonal.

• Closed-bottom sport zippers work best for the Extender Tote and the Weekender that call for separating zippers. Separating zippers can be adapted for use in other projects.

• When using upholstery fabric, it will sometimes be necessary to use a lining fabric. The stripe upholstery fabric in this set is not lined, whereas the brown has a rubberized backing and needs to be lined.

• When aligning the loop tape with the hook tape, drop the loop tape down ⅛" lower than the hook tape to keep it from showing on the outside.

Sizes & Materials for Entire Set

PROJECT SPECIFICATIONS

Air Travel Bag: 15¾" x 12¼" x 5"
Companion Purse: 9¾" x 7" x 2½"
Mini Pocket Purse: 7¾" x 4¼" x 1"
Extender Tote: Approximately 17¾" x 12½" x 5¼"
The Weekender: 18¾" x 16" x 6¼"
Handy Wallet: 7¾" x 11¾" open and 7¾" x 4" closed (includes binding)
Barrel Bag: Approximately 18" x 8"

MATERIALS FOR ENTIRE SET

- ¼ yard 42"-wide non-quilted coordinating fabric with body for inside pockets of wallet
- ⅔ yard 56"-wide lightweight brown upholstery fabric
- 1⅝ yards 42"-wide coordinating lining fabric
- 2⅛ yards 42"-wide double-sided quilted fabric
- 2¼ yards 56"-wide medium-weight brown-and-tan stripe upholstery fabric

SUPPLIES & TOOLS FOR ENTIRE SET

- All-purpose thread to match fabrics
- 1 each 9", 16" and 18" brown closed-bottom sport zippers
- 1 (7") cream closed-bottom sport zipper
- 1 (18") brown separating sport zipper
- 2 (26") cream separating sport zippers
- 2 (7") cream closed-bottom zippers for wallet
- 18" length ⅝"-wide hook-and-loop tape
- 19" length ⅜"-wide cream grosgrain ribbon for zipper pulls
- 25" length ⅜"-wide brown grosgrain ribbon for zipper pulls
- 25" length ⅞"-wide cream grosgrain ribbon for wallet binding
- ½"–¾" flat brown button (optional)
- Zipper foot
- Basic sewing tools and supplies

Pattern Layout & Cutting for Entire Set

Brown-and-Tan Stripe

***Note:** Refer to Figure 1 for cutting layout for best use of fabric.*

1. Cut two 16½" x 15½" A rectangles for the body of the Air Travel Bag; cut a 2⅜" square from both bottom corners referring to Figure 1 for cutout positioning.

2. Cut one 16½" x 8¾" B rectangle for Air Travel Bag outside pocket; cut a 2⅜" square from both bottom corners, again referring to Figure 1 for cutout positioning.

3. Cut one 6" x 20" C rectangle for Air Travel Bag outside center pocket.

4. Cut two 5¼" x 9¾" D rectangles for Air Travel Bag outside right and left side pockets; cut a 2⅜" square out of one bottom corner on the left side of one D and on the right side of the second D, again referring to Figure 1 for positioning.

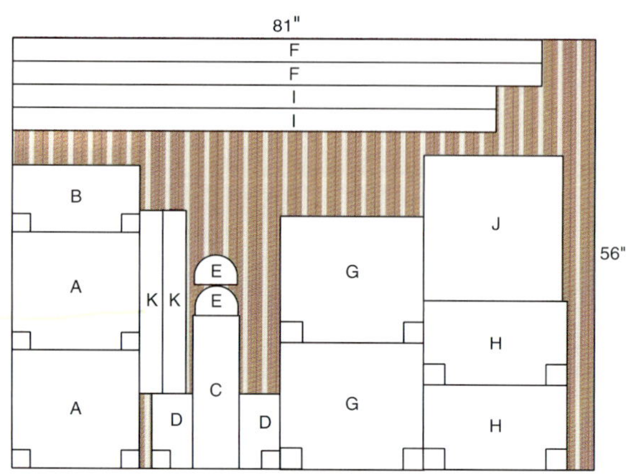

Figure 1

5. Prepare template for E (see page 15); cut as directed on pattern.

6. Cut two 3" x 68" F strips for Air Travel Bag straps.

7. Cut two 18½" x 16½" G rectangles for the body of the Extender Tote; cut a 2¾" square from both bottom corners, again referring to Figure 1 for positioning.

8. Cut two 18½" x 11" H rectangles for Extender Tote outside pockets; cut a 2¾" square from both bottom corners, again referring to Figure 1 for positioning.

9. Cut two 3" x 62" I strips for Extender Tote straps.

10. Cut one 19" x 17¾" J rectangle for Barrel Bag.

11. Cut two 3" x 24" K strips for Barrel Bag straps.

Brown Upholstery Fabric

Note: *Refer to Figure 2 for cutting layout for best use of fabric.*

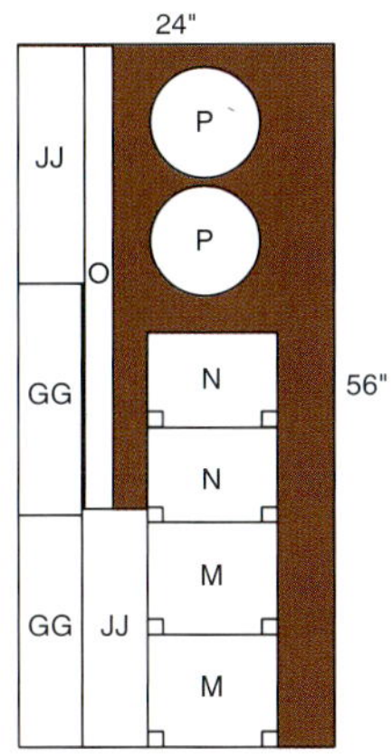

Figure 2

1. Cut two 18½" x 5" GG rectangles for Extender Tote extender.

2. Cut two 10½" x 9" M rectangles for Companion Purse; cut a 1¼" square from both bottom corners referring to Figure 2 for positioning.

3. Cut two 10½" x 7½" N rectangles for Companion Purse outside pockets; cut a 1¼" square from both bottom corners referring to Figure 2 for positioning.

4. Cut one 2" x 37" O strip for Companion Purse strap.

5. Cut two 19" x 5¼" JJ rectangles for Barrel Bag.

6. Prepare template for P using pattern given on page 25; cut as directed on the piece for Barrel Bag ends.

Lining Fabric

Note: *Refer to Figure 3 for cutting layout for best use of fabric.*

1. Cut two 16½" x 9¾" AIP rectangles for Air Travel Bag inside pocket linings; cut a 2⅜" square from both bottom corners referring to Figure 3 for positioning.

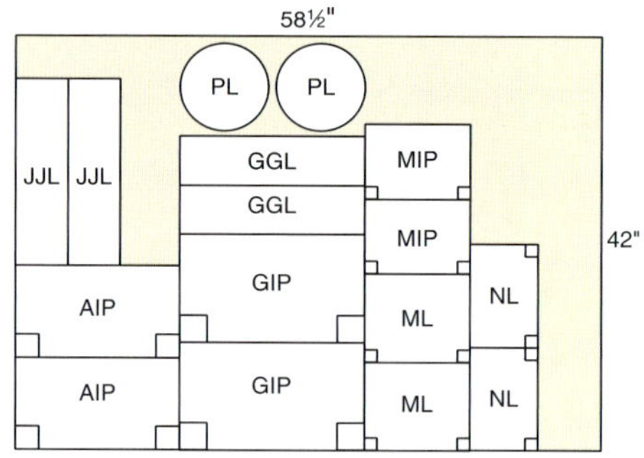

Figure 3

2. Cut two 18½" x 11" GIP rectangles for Extender Tote inside pocket linings; cut a 2¾" square from both bottom corners referring to Figure 3 for positioning.

3. Cut two 18½" x 5" GGL rectangles for Extender Tote extender lining.

4. Cut two 10½" x 9" ML rectangles for Companion Purse lining; cut a 1¼" square from both bottom corners referring to Figure 3 for positioning.

5. Cut two 10½" x 6¾" NL rectangles for Companion Purse outside pocket lining; cut a 1¼" square from both bottom corners referring to Figure 3 for positioning.

6. Cut two 10½" x 7½" MIP rectangles for Companion Purse N outside pocket linings; cut a 1¼" square from both bottom corners referring to Figure 3 for positioning.

7. Cut two 19" x 5¼" JJL rectangles for Barrel Bag lining.

8. Cut two P circles using pattern given for Barrel Bag end linings.

Quilted Fabric

Note: *Refer to Figure 4 for cutting layout for best use of fabric.*

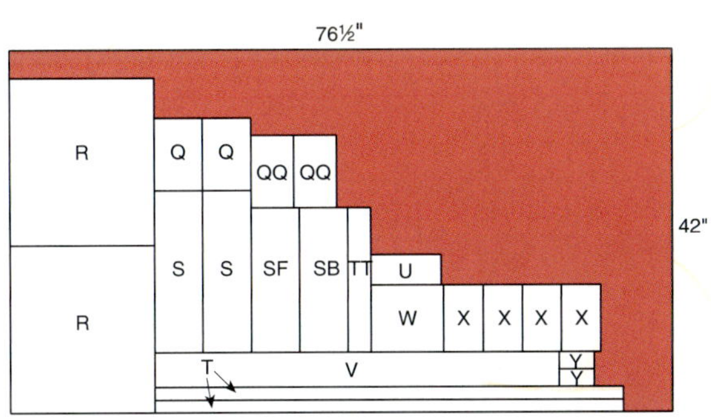

Figure 4

1. Cut two 8½" x 5½" Q rectangles for Mini Pocket Purse.

2. Cut two 8½" x 5" QQ pocket pieces for Mini Pocket Purse.

3. Cut two 19½" x 16¾" R rectangles for the body of The Weekender.

4. Cut two 5½" x 18¾" S rectangles for The Weekender side panels.

5. Cut two 5½" x 16¾" strips for The Weekender front and back side panels; label one strip SF and one SB.

6. Cut two 1½" x 53½" T zipper strips for The Weekender.

7. Cut one 2¾" x 16¾" TT back zipper strip for The Weekender.

8. Cut one 3½" x 8" U strip for The Weekender handle.

9. Cut one 4" x 46" optional V strip for The Weekender strap.

10. Cut one 7¾" x 8¼" W rectangle for Handy Wallet top outside.

11. Cut four 7¾" x 4½" X rectangles and label X1, X2, X3 and X4 for Handy Wallet pockets.

12. Cut two 2" x 4" Y rectangles for Handy Wallet strap.

Non-Quilted Coordinating Fabric

1. Cut three 7¾" x 4½" WIP rectangles for Handy Wallet inside pockets referring to Figure 5. ■

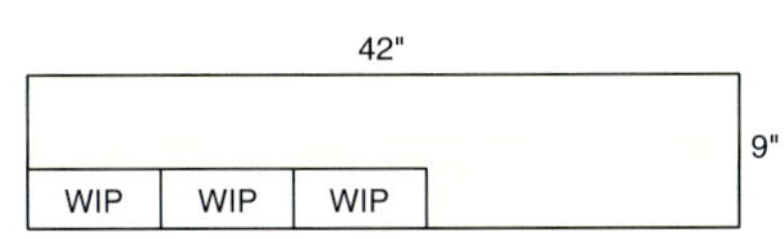

Figure 5

Air Travel Bag

Make use of the multiple pockets on the outside and inside of this bag for organizing your travel items.

PROJECT NOTES

If you have already cut the pieces for this bag as part of the set, proceed to Assembly Instructions.

PROJECT SPECIFICATIONS

Bag Size: 15¾" x 12¼" x 5"

MATERIALS

- ⅜ yard 42"-wide coordinating lining fabric
- 2 yards 56"-wide medium-weight brown-and-tan stripe upholstery fabric

SUPPLIES & TOOLS

- All-purpose thread to match fabric
- 16" brown closed-bottom sport zipper
- 4 (2") lengths ⅝"-wide hook-and-loop tape
- 6" length ⅜"-wide brown grosgrain ribbon for zipper pull
- ½"–¾" flat brown button (optional)
- Zipper foot
- Basic sewing tools and supplies

Cutting

***Note:** Refer to Figure 1 for cutting in steps 1–6 for best use of brown-and-tan stripe fabric and positioning pieces on stripes.*

1. Cut two 16½" x 15½" A rectangles for the body of the bag; cut a 2⅜" square from both bottom corners referring to Figure 1 for cutout positioning.

2. Cut one 16½" x 9¾" B rectangle for outside pocket; cut a 2⅜" square from both bottom corners, again referring to Figure 1 for cutout positioning.

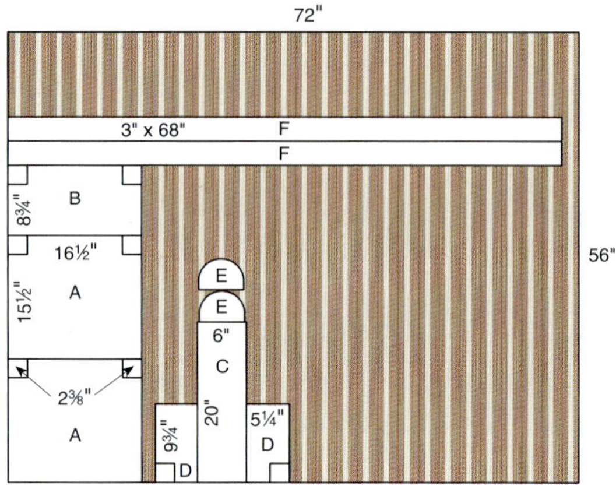

Figure 1

3. Cut one 6" x 20" C rectangle for outside center pocket.

4. Cut two 5¼" x 9¾" D rectangles for outside right and left side pockets; cut a 2⅜" square from one bottom corner on the left side of one D and on the right side of the second D, again referring to Figure 1 for positioning.

5. Prepare template for E; cut as directed on pattern.

6. Cut two 3" x 68" F strips for straps.

7. Cut two 16½" x 9¾" AIP rectangles for inside pocket linings; cut a 2⅜" square from both bottom corners of each rectangle referring to Figure 2 for positioning.

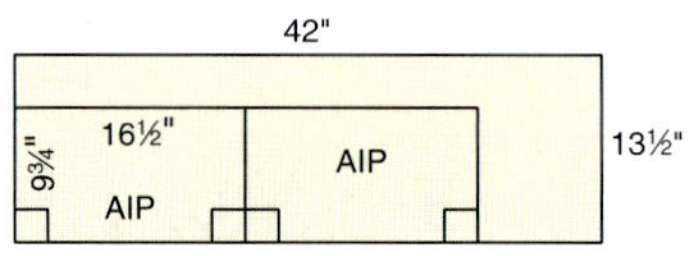

Figure 2

PASSPORT
PASSPORT
United States
of America

Assembly Instructions

Note: *Use a ⅜" seam allowance throughout unless otherwise noted.*

1. Join F strips on short ends to make a tube; press seams open.

2. Fold and press ⅜" to the wrong side along one long side and ½" on the other long side of the stitched tube.

3. Fold the pressed tube with wrong sides together, matching pressed edges; stitch ⅛" from the open edge and ⅛" from the folded edge as shown in Figure 3 to complete the strap; set aside.

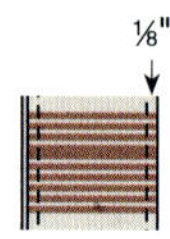

Figure 3

4. Using a zigzag stitch, center and stitch one strip of hook tape to the right side of one E pocket flap piece, 1" above bottom curved edge as shown in Figure 4.

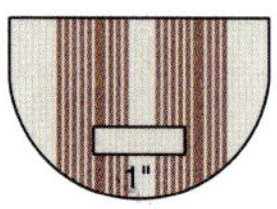

Figure 4

5. With the right sides of the E flaps together, sew side and curved edges together; clip corners and curved edges as shown in Figure 5. Press seams open. Turn the pocket flap right side out; press flat and serge top edge.

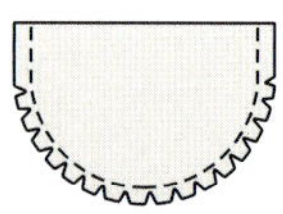

Figure 5

6. Topstitch ¼" from edges of flap around curved edges as shown in Figure 6. ***Note:*** *If using the optional button, center and sew the button 1" from the bottom of the curved edge on the side without the hook tape.* Set aside.

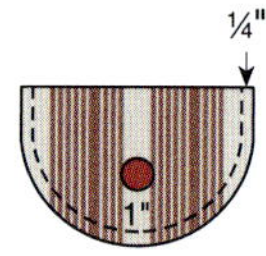

Figure 6

7. Serge across one 6" edge of C. With the wrong side of the fabric facing up, fold the C piece back 12¾" from the unstitched edge of C; press. Fold up 3" from the first fold as shown in Figure 7; press.

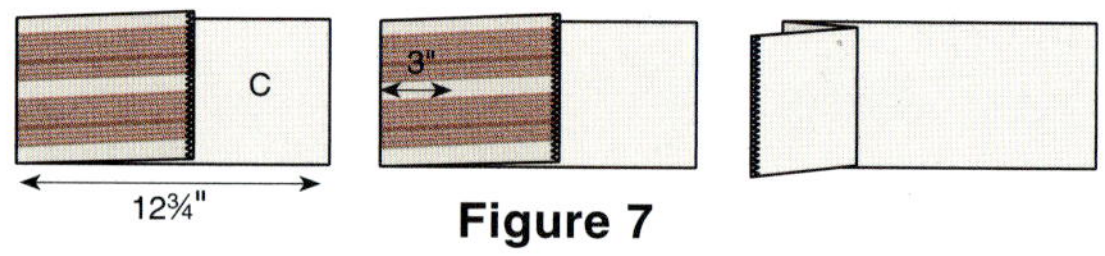

Figure 7

8. Turn the C piece over with right side facing up; lay the second fold back out of the way. Using a zigzag stitch, center and stitch one strip of loop tape 1" down from first fold on the outside of the C pocket piece, stitching through two layers of fabric as shown in Figure 8.

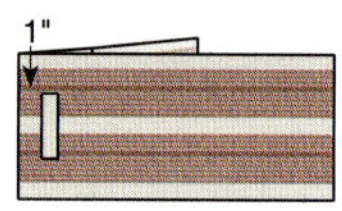

Figure 8

9. Align and center the straight edge of E at the top of C; using a zigzag stitch, center and stitch one strip of hook tape to the top of the E-C panel on three sides as shown in Figure 9.

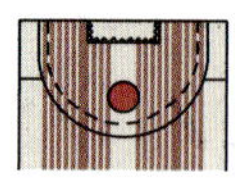

Figure 9

10. Fold the top of the E-C panel under ⅝" and stitch in place as shown in Figure 10. Fold the E pocket flap down, aligning the hook tape with the loop tape; set aside.

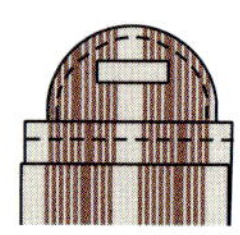

Figure 10

11. Using a serger or zigzag stitch, sew along the top edge of B, D and each AIP piece. ***Note:*** *The top edge is opposite the corner cutout edge.*

12. Center and zigzag-stitch three edges of one strip of the hook tape to the right-side top edge of one D and one AIP piece as shown in Figure 11.

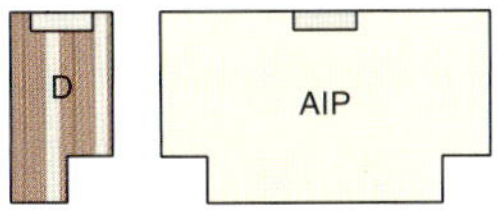

Figure 11

13. Fold under a ⅝" hem on the top edge of each B, D and AIP piece; press. Stitch in place close to the serged or zigzagged edge.

14. Pin the D pocket pieces to the right side of one A piece, matching bottom raw edges and cutout corners as shown in Figure 12 and photo below.

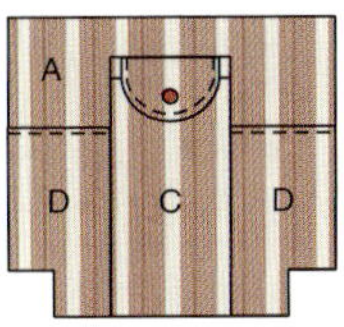

Figure 12

15. Pin the C pocket piece to the right side of A between the two D pockets, again referring to Figure 12; fold back the top edges of the C piece and the D piece with hook tape. Align loop tape on A with the hook tape on C and D; zigzag-stitch loop pieces in place.

16. Align the AIP piece without the hook tape with the bottom and sides on the wrong side of the A-C-D panel, aligning cutout corners; machine-stitch across the bottom of the panel ⅜" above the cutout corners as shown in Figure 13.

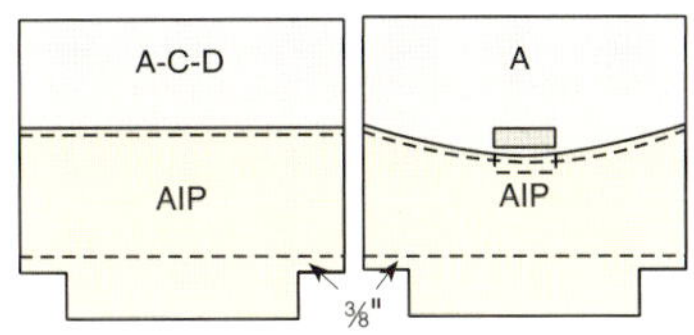

Figure 13

17. Pin the remaining AIP piece with hook tape to the back side of the remaining A piece. Align loop tape with the hook tape and zigzag-stitch in place, again referring to Figure 13.

Add C and D pocket pieces to create special-sized pockets to make air travel easier.

18. Pin B to the right side of the A-AIP panel, matching bottom edges; machine-stitch across the panel ⅜" above the cutout corners as shown in Figure 14.

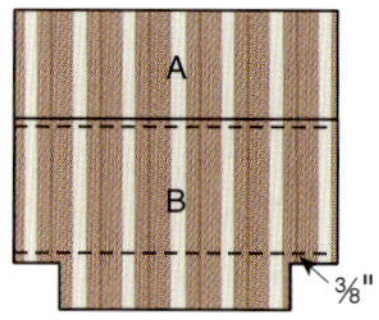

Figure 14

This A-B-AIP panel has pockets on both sides.

19. Using a serger or zigzag stitch, stitch all edges of each A-B-AIP and A-C-D-AIP panel, leaving cutout sections until last as shown in Figure 15.

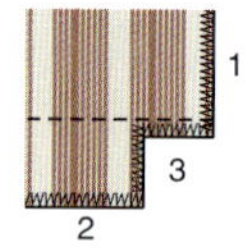

Figure 15

20. With right sides together, join the two A-B and A-C-D panels at the bottom edge as shown in Figure 16; press seam open. Stitch ¼" on each side of the seam line to hold seam allowance in place, again referring to Figure 16.

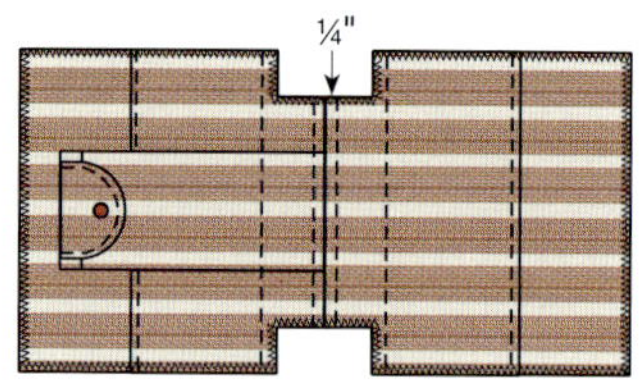

Figure 16

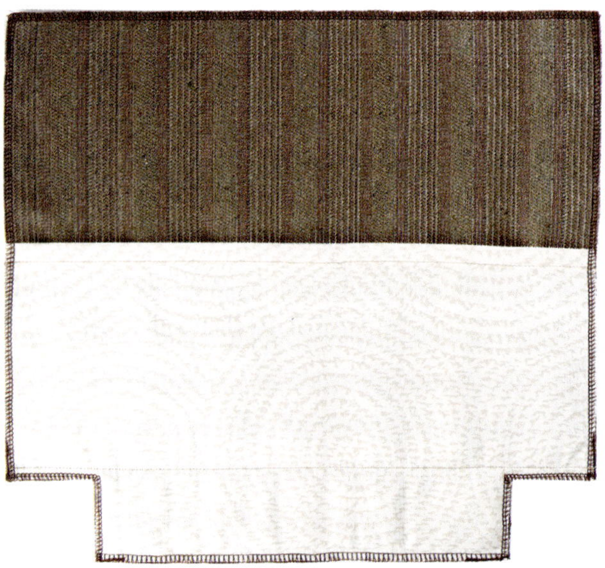

This is the inside of the A-B panel.

This is the inside of the A-C-D panel.

Straps that go all the way around the bottom make this a very sturdy bag. See step 21 for instructions on sewing straps to panel.

21. Lay the stitched panel right side up on a flat surface. Pin and stitch the strap in place, aligning it with the outer edges of the E pocket flap, matching seams on strap with the bottom seam of the bag and ending 2¼" from the top edge as shown in Figure 17 and the photo on page 13. Sew an X at the top of each strip, again referring to Figure 17.

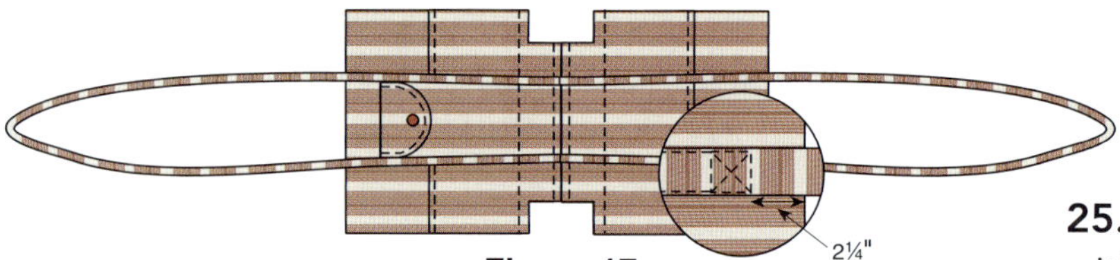

Figure 17

22. Mark in ¾" from side edges at the end of each panel; open zipper and lay face down on the right side of one panel end even with the top edge, placing the open end of the zipper at the ¾" mark. Using a zipper foot, stitch a ⅜" seam between the ¾" marks to attach the zipper tape as shown in Figure 18.

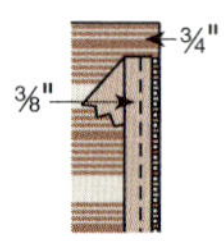

Figure 18

23. Fold the zipper tape to the inside and topstitch ¼" from top edge of panel; repeat on the other side of the zipper on the other end of the panel. ***Note:*** *If using a separating zipper, sew a bar tack at the end to keep it from separating.*

24. With right sides together, pin side edges together and stitch as shown in Figure 19; press seams open. Fold zipper tape back on an angle at the zipper open end; stitch in place on topstitching line, again referring to Figure 19.

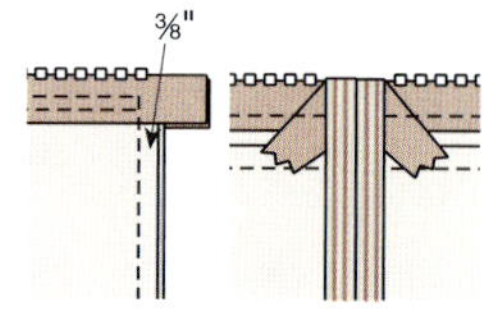

Figure 19

25. With right sides together, align side seam with bottom seam on one bottom corner and stitch across edge as shown in Figure 20 to make square bottom corner. Repeat on other bottom corner of bag. Turn bag right side out.

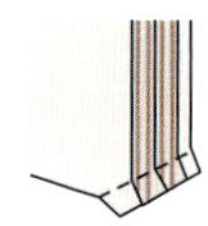

Figure 20

26. Fold the 6" strip of ⅜"-wide grosgrain ribbon in half to make a 3" double loop; push folded end through the zipper tab, forming a loop. Pull ends of ribbon through the loop as shown in Figure 21; cut ends diagonally to finish. ■

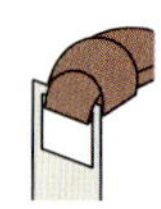

Figure 21

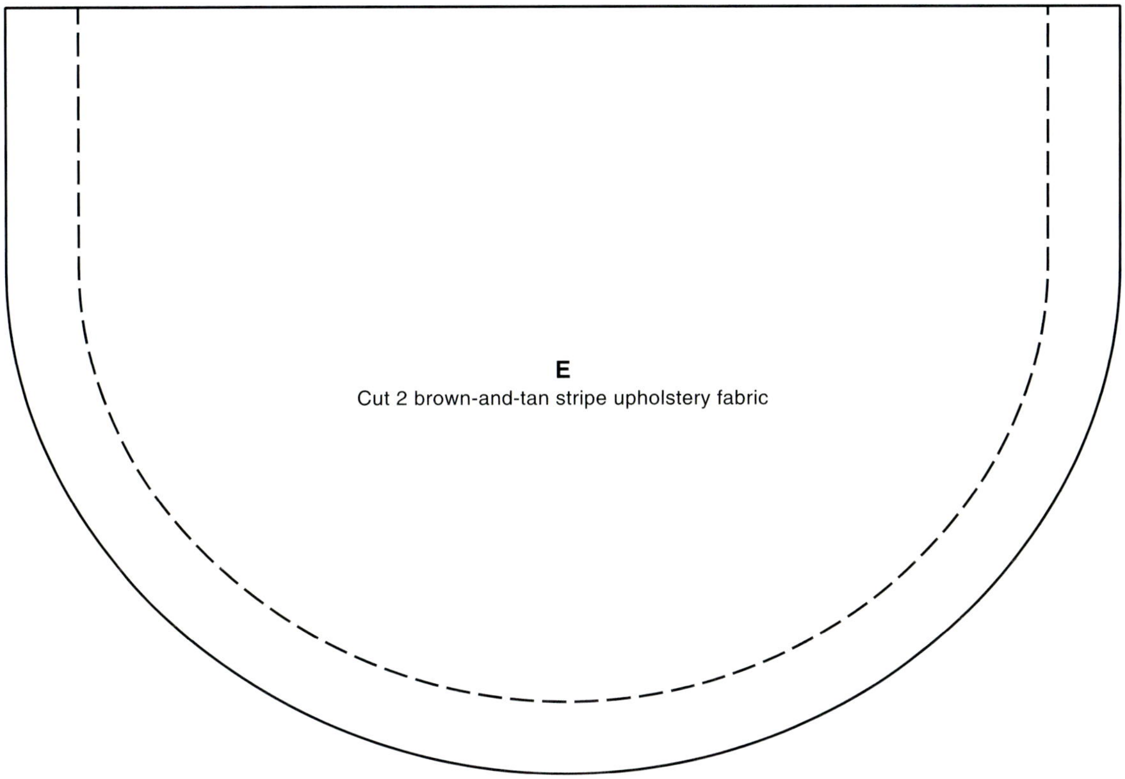

Air Travel Bag
Placement Diagram
15¾" x 12¼" x 5"

Companion Purse

Make a companion purse with a handy shoulder strap to coordinate with your travel bags.

PROJECT NOTES
If you have already cut the pieces for this purse as part of the set, proceed to the Assembly Instructions.

PROJECT SPECIFICATIONS
Purse Size: 9¾" x 7" x 2½"

MATERIALS
- ½ yard 56"-wide lightweight brown upholstery fabric
- ⅝ yard 42"-wide coordinating lining fabric

SUPPLIES & TOOLS
- All-purpose thread to match fabric
- 9" brown closed-bottom sport zipper
- 2 (2") lengths ⅝"-wide hook-and-loop tape
- 6" length ⅜"-wide brown grosgrain ribbon for zipper pull
- Zipper foot
- Basic sewing tools and supplies

Cutting
1. Cut two 10½" x 9" M rectangles lightweight brown upholstery fabric; cut a 1¼" square from both bottom corners referring to Figure 1 for positioning.

2. Cut two 10½" x 7½" N rectangles lightweight brown upholstery fabric for outside pockets; cut a 1¼" square from both bottom corners, again referring to Figure 1 for positioning.

3. Cut one 2" x 37" O strip lightweight brown upholstery fabric for strap.

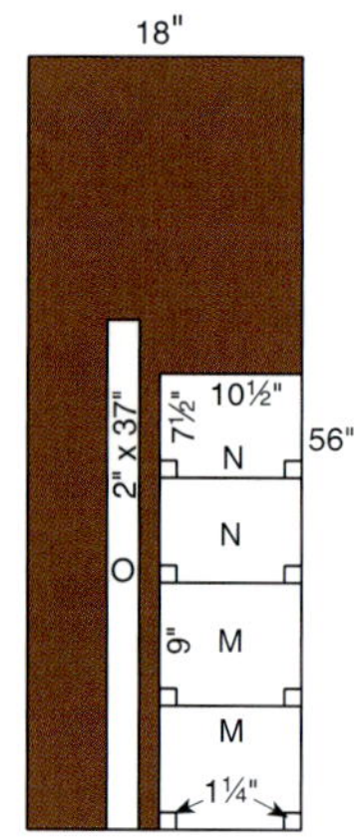

Figure 1

4. Cut two 10½" x 9" ML rectangles coordinating lining fabric; cut a 1¼" square from both bottom corners referring to Figure 2 for positioning.

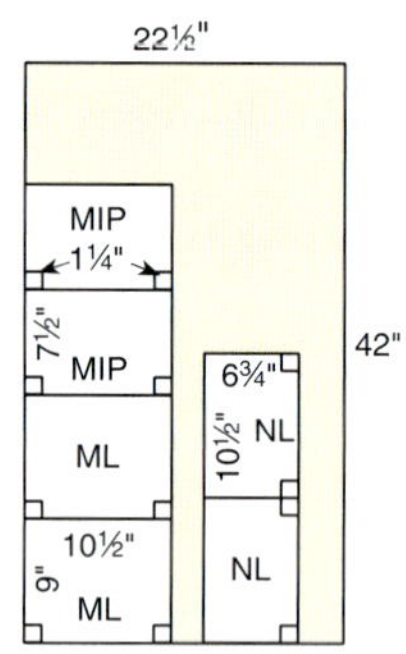

Figure 2

5. Cut two 10½" x 6¾" NL rectangles coordinating lining fabric for outside pocket lining; cut a 1¼" square from both bottom corners, again referring to Figure 2 for positioning.

6. Cut two 10½" x 7½" MIP rectangles coordinating lining fabric for inside pocket lining;

cut a 1¼" square from both bottom corners, again referring to Figure 2 for positioning.

Assembly Instructions

Note: *Use a ⅜" seam allowance throughout unless otherwise noted.*

1. Serge or zigzag across the end of each O strap.

2. Fold and press ⅜" to the wrong side along one long side and ½" on the other long side of O.

3. Fold the pressed O strip with wrong sides together, matching pressed edges; stitch ⅛" from the folded edge as shown in Figure 3 to complete the strap; set aside.

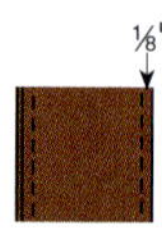

Figure 3

4. Serge or zigzag along the long top edge of each N and MIP piece.

5. Using a zigzag stitch, center and stitch three sides of one strip of hook tape to the right side of the top edge of one N and one MIP as shown in Figure 4.

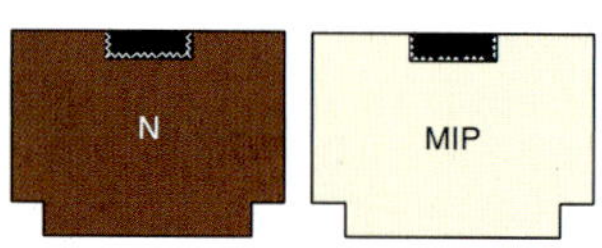

Figure 4

6. Pin an NL piece to the wrong side of each N piece, matching bottom raw edges and cutout corners; fold down a ⅝" hem over the lining on the top edge of each N piece and press. Machine-stitch close to the serged or zigzagged edge to hem as shown in Figure 5.

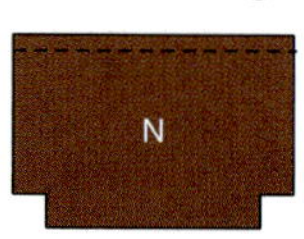

Figure 5

Notice how the hook-and-loop tape is aligned and stitched to the lining.

Hook-and-loop tape holds items securely in the outside pocket of the purse.

If your thread matches the fabric the stitching on the outside pocket lines disappears into the fabric.

You can vary the size of the side pockets to fit your needs.

7. Fold down a ⅝" hem on the top of the MIP pieces; press. Machine-stitch to hem as in step 6.

8. With wrong sides together, using a serger or zigzag stitch, join M and ML at the top edges. Pin sides and bottom edges together.

9. Pin the N-NL outside pocket piece with the hook tape to the outside of one M-ML panel, matching bottom edges and cutout corners. Fold back the top edge of the N pocket with the hook tape; align the loop tape on M with the hook tape on N and zigzag loop tape in place referring to Figure 6. Repeat the process with MIP on the ML side of the second M-ML panel.

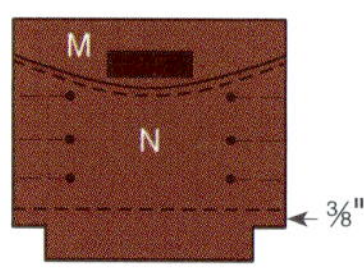

Figure 6

10. Pin the remaining N-MIP pockets in place on the outside and inside of the M-ML panels, matching raw edges and cutout corners. Machine-stitch across the bottom of each panel ⅜" above the cutout corners, again referring to Figure 6.

11. Stitch pocket lines on the M-N panels as shown in Figure 7. ***Note:*** *The pockets in the purse shown are sewn 3" in from side edges. You may vary this according to your needs.*

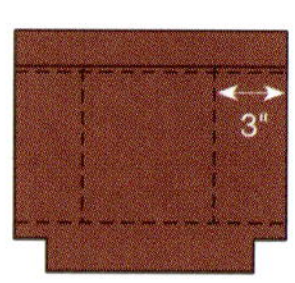

Figure 7

12. Serge or zigzag remaining edges of M-N panels, leaving cutout sections until last as shown in Figure 8.

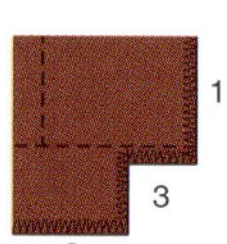

Figure 8

13. Mark in ¾" from side edges at the top edge of each M-N panel; open zipper and lay face down on the right side of one panel end even with top edge, placing the open end of zipper at the ¾" mark. Using the zipper foot, stitch a ⅜" seam between the ¾" marks to attach zipper tape.

14. Fold zipper tape to the inside and topstitch ¼" from top edge of panel; repeat with the other side of the zipper on the top of the other panel.

15. With right sides together, pin the panel side edges together and stitch as shown in Figure 9; press seams open.

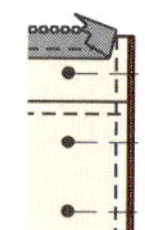
Figure 9

16. Push one end of the O strap through the opening at the closed end of the zipper, extending the strap 1" inside; machine-stitch securely into the seam as shown in Figure 10.

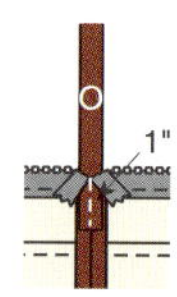

Figure 10

17. With right sides together, join the two M-N panels at the bottom edge; press seam open and stitch ¼" on each side of the seam line to hold seam allowance in place as shown in Figure 11.

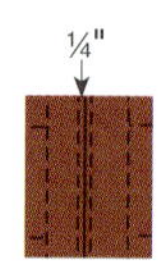

Figure 11

18. Machine-stitch the remaining sides of the M-N panels together; press seam open. Fold and pin zipper tape back at an angle at the zipper open end; position the remaining end of the O strip 1" inside the bag and machine-stitch on seam line. Stitch zipper tape on topstitching line as shown in Figure 12.

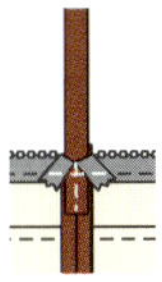

Figure 12

19. With right sides together, align side seam with bottom seam on one end and stitch across the bottom/side seam as shown in Figure 13 to make a square bottom corner; repeat on other end of bag. Turn bag right side out.

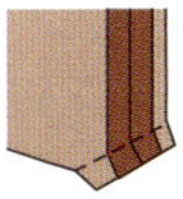

Figure 13

Figure 14

20. Fold the 6" strip of ⅜"-wide grosgrain ribbon in half to make a 3" double strip; push folded edge through the zipper tab, forming a loop. Pull ends of ribbon through loop as shown in Figure 14; cut ends diagonally. ■

Companion Purse
Placement Diagram
9¾" x 7" x 2½"

Barrel Bag

Stitch this Barrel Bag to carry shoes or other heavier items when you travel.

PROJECT NOTES
If you have already cut the pieces for the bag as part of the set, proceed to Assembly Instructions.

PROJECT SPECIFICATIONS
Bag Size: Approximately 18" x 8"

MATERIALS
- ⅓ yard 56"-wide lightweight brown upholstery fabric
- ½ yard 42"-wide coordinating lining fabric
- ⅝ yard 56"-wide medium-weight brown-and-tan stripe upholstery fabric

SUPPLIES & TOOLS
- All-purpose thread to match fabric
- 18" brown closed-bottom sport zipper
- 6" length ⅜"-wide brown grosgrain ribbon for zipper pull
- Zipper foot
- Basic sewing tools and supplies

Cutting
Note: *Refer to Figure 1 for placement for cutting brown-and-tan stripe upholstery fabric.*

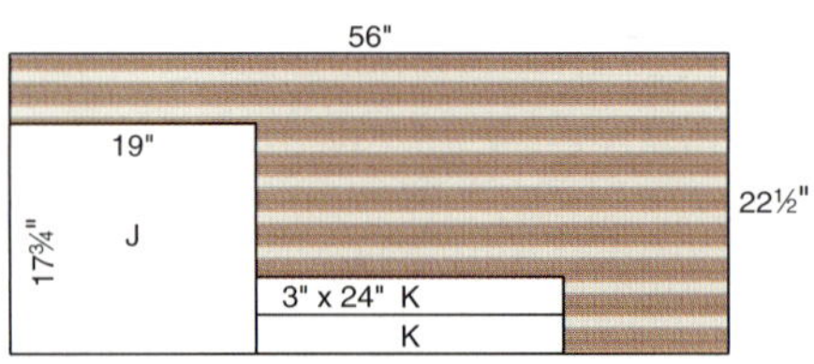

Figure 1

1. Cut one 19" x 17¾" J rectangle brown-and-tan stripe.

2. Cut two 3" x 24" K strips brown-and-tan stripe for straps.

3. Cut two 19" x 5¼" JJ rectangles lightweight brown upholstery fabric.

4. Prepare template for P using pattern given; cut as directed on the piece.

5. Cut two 19" x 5¼" JJL rectangles lining fabric.

Assembly Instructions
Note: *Use a ⅜" seam allowance throughout unless otherwise noted.*

1. Serge or zigzag ends of each K piece. Fold and press ⅜" to the wrong side along one long side and ½" along the other long side. Fold the fabric wrong sides together, matching pressed edges. Stitch ⅛" from open edge and ⅛" from folded edge as shown in Figure 2 to complete handles; set aside.

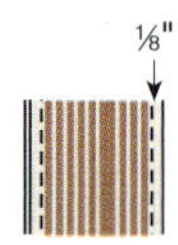

Figure 2

2. Layer a JJ piece with a JJL piece with wrong sides together; serge or zigzag all edges. Repeat with remaining JJ and JJL and P and PL pieces.

3. Mark ½" from side edges at the end of each JJ-JJL panel; open zipper and lay right side down on the right side of fabric even with the top edge, placing the open end of the zipper at the ½" mark. Using a zipper foot, stitch a ⅜" seam from one end of the panel to the other to attach zipper tape.

4. Fold zipper tape to the inside and topstitch ¼"

HOUSE OF WHITE BIRCHES, BERNE, INDIANA 46711 DRGNETWORK.COM

from top edge of panel; repeat on the other side of the zipper on the second panel. ***Note:*** *If using a separating zipper, sew a bar tack at the end to keep it from separating.*

5. Measure out from the center bottom of each JJ panel 2½"; position the serged ends of a K strap as shown in Figure 3 and baste in place.

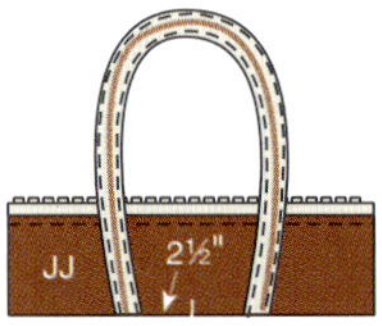

Figure 3

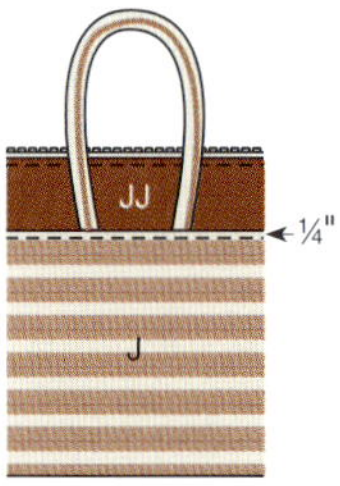

Figure 4

6. With right sides together, join the bottom edge of one JJ panel to one long edge of the J piece; press seam toward J. Topstitch ¼" from top of J as shown in Figure 4. Repeat on the other end of J.

Using a light-colored lining makes it easier to find items in this sports bag.

7. Fold each P-PL panel in half vertically and horizontally and pin to mark centers to divide in quarters as shown in Figure 5.

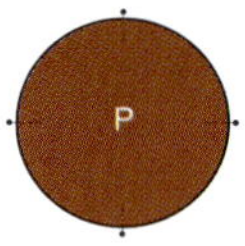

Figure 5

8. Starting with the opening end of the zipper, with right sides together, join P-PL and J-JJ panels together as shown in Figure 6. Reinforce seam with a second row of stitching ⅛" outside the first row, again referring to Figure 6. Unzip zipper, press seams toward the P-PL panel. Repeat the process at the other end of the J-JJ panel. Turn bag right side out.

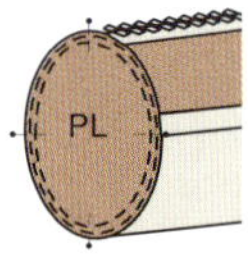

Figure 6

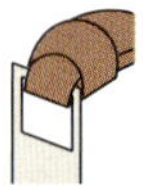
Figure 7

9. Fold the 6" strip of ⅜"-wide grosgrain ribbon in half to make a 3" double strip; push folded edge through the zipper tab, forming a loop. Pull ends of ribbon through loop as shown in Figure 7; cut ends diagonally. ■

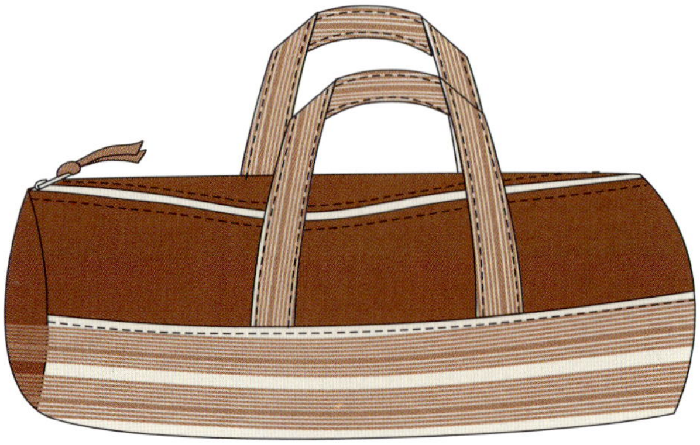

Barrel Bag
Placement Diagram
Approximately 18" x 8"

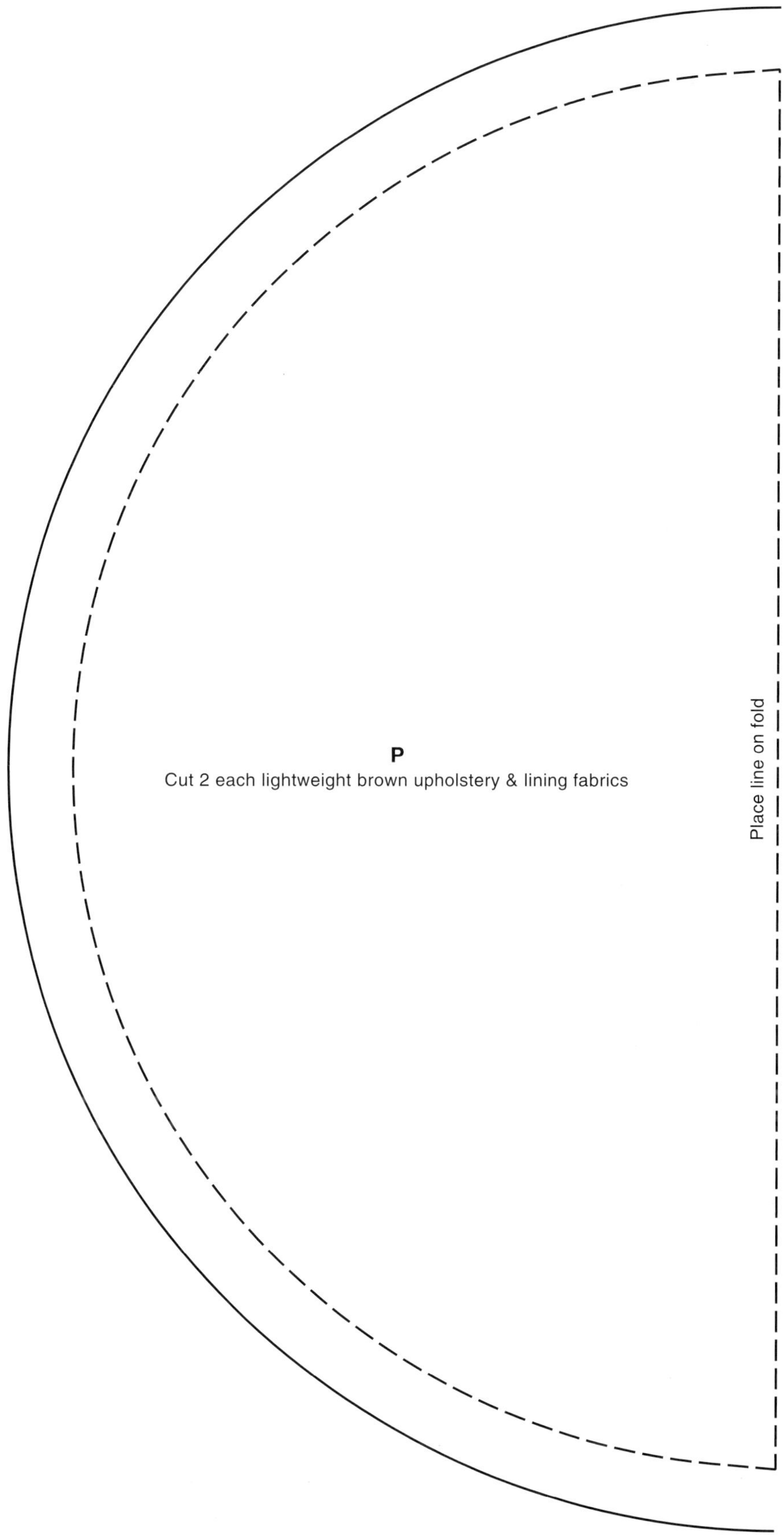
P
Cut 2 each lightweight brown upholstery & lining fabrics
Place line on fold

Extender Tote

Similar to the Air Travel Bag, this Extender Tote has added pieces in the top opening to expand the bag to hold more for your travel convenience.

PROJECT NOTES

If you have already cut the pieces for this Extender Tote as part of the set, proceed to Assembly Instructions.

PROJECT SPECIFICATIONS

Bag Size: Approximately 17¾" x 12½" x 5¼"

MATERIALS

- ¼ yard 56"-wide lightweight brown upholstery fabric
- ⅝ yard 42"-wide coordinating lining fabric
- 1⅞ yards 56"-wide medium-weight brown-and-tan stripe upholstery fabric

SUPPLIES & TOOLS

- All-purpose thread to match fabric
- 18" brown separating sport zipper
- 2 (2") lengths ⅝"-wide hook-and-loop tape
- 6" length ⅜"-wide brown grosgrain ribbon for zipper pull
- Zipper foot
- Basic sewing tools and supplies

Cutting

1. Cut two 18½" x 16½" G rectangles brown-and-tan stripe; cut a 2¾" square from both bottom corners, again referring to Figure 1 for positioning.

2. Cut two 18½" x 11" H rectangles brown-and-tan stripe outside pockets; cut a 2¾" square from both bottom corners, again referring to Figure 1 for positioning.

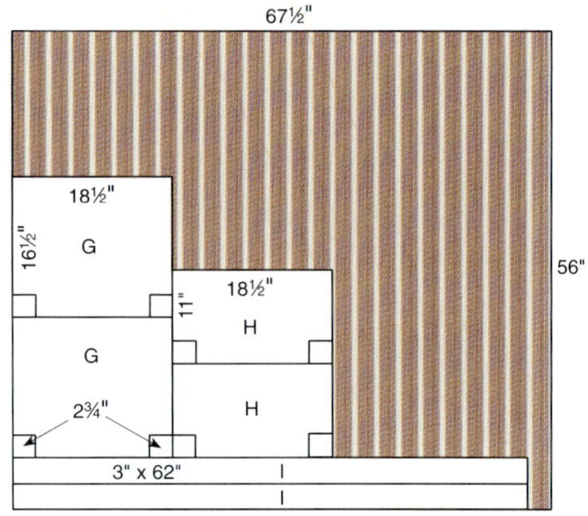

Figure 1

3. Cut two 3" x 62" I strips brown-and-tan stripe for straps.

4. Cut two 18½" x 5" GG rectangles lightweight brown upholstery fabric for extender.

5. Cut two 18½" x 11" GIP rectangles lining fabric for inside pockets; cut a 2¾" square from both bottom corners referring to Figure 2 for positioning.

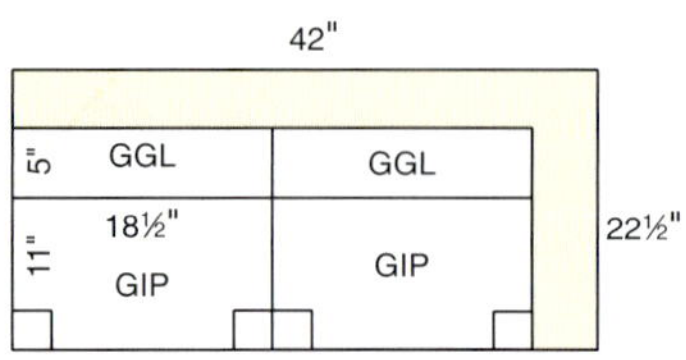

Figure 2

6. Cut two 18½" x 5" GGL rectangles lining fabric for extender lining.

Assembly Instructions

Note: *Use a ⅜" seam allowance throughout unless otherwise noted.*

ITORS GUIDE
VILLAGE

1. Join ends of I strips to make a tube; press seams open.

2. Fold and press ⅜" to the wrong side along one long side and ½" on the other long side of the stitched tube.

3. Fold the pressed tube with wrong sides together, matching pressed edges; stitch ⅛" from the open edge and ⅛" from the folded edge as shown in Figure 3 to complete the strap; set aside.

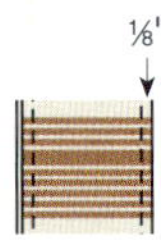

Figure 3

4. Using a serger or zigzag stitch, sew along the top edge of each H and GIP piece.

5. Using a zigzag stitch, center and stitch three sides of one strip of hook tape to the top right side of one each H and GIP pieces.

6. Fold under a ⅝" hem on the top edge of each H and GIP pocket piece; press. Stitch close to serged edges as shown in Figure 4.

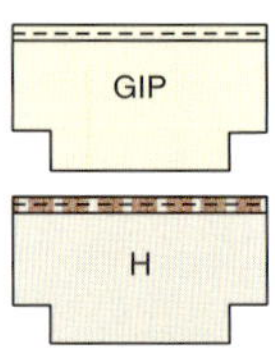

Figure 4

7. Pin the H pocket with the hook tape to the right side of one G panel, matching bottom raw edges and cutout corners. Fold back the top edge of the H pocket; align the loop tape on G with the hook tape. Zigzag loop tape in place referring to Figure 5.

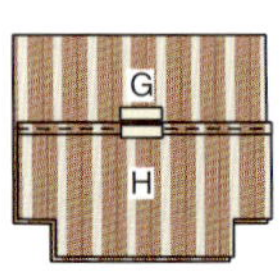

Figure 5

8. Pin the GIP pocket with the hook tape to the inside of the remaining G panel, matching bottom raw edges and cutout corners; zigzag loop tape in place on the wrong side of the G panel.

9. Pin the remaining H piece to the outside of the G panel with the GIP pocket piece, matching bottom raw edges and cutout corners. Pin the remaining GIP pocket to the inside of the remaining G-H panel. Machine-stitch across bottom of each panel ⅜" above the cutout corners as shown in Figure 6.

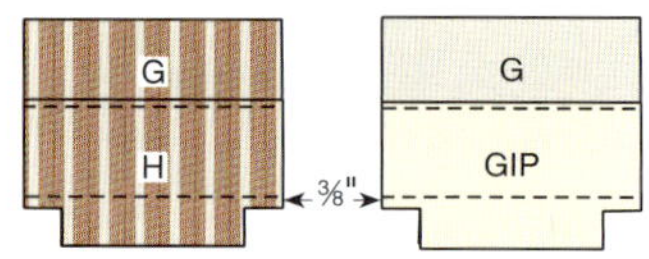

Figure 6

10. Serge or zigzag all edges of each panel, leaving cutout sections until last as shown in Figure 7; set aside.

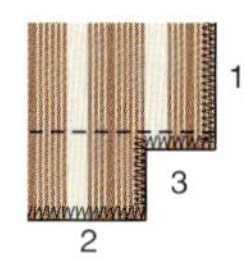

Figure 7

11. Lay a GG piece wrong sides together with a GGL piece; serge or zigzag edges together all around.

12. Mark in ¾" from side edges of each GG-GGL panel; open zipper and lay face down on the right side of one panel's finished edge even with the top edge, placing the open end of the zipper at the ¾" mark. Using a zipper foot, stitch a ⅜" seam between the ¾" marks to attach zipper tape as shown in Figure 8. ***Note:*** *The end of the zipper teeth will extend beyond the ¾" mark.*

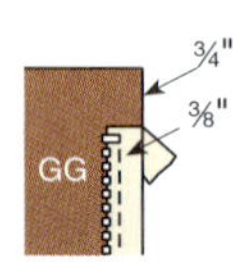

Figure 8

13. Fold zipper tape to the inside and topstitch ¼" from top edge of panel; repeat the process with the other side of the zipper on the remaining GG-GGL panel.

14. With right sides together, join the bottom edges of the GG-GGL panels to the top edges of the G-H panels, aligning the side edges as shown in Figure 9; press seams open.

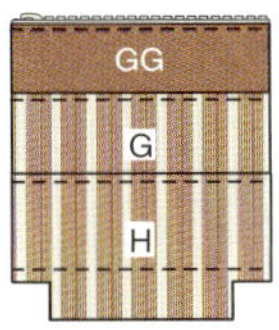

Figure 9

15. With right sides together, join the two G-GIP panels at the bottom edge as shown in Figure 10; stitch ¼" on each side of the seam line to hold seam allowance in place, again referring to Figure 10.

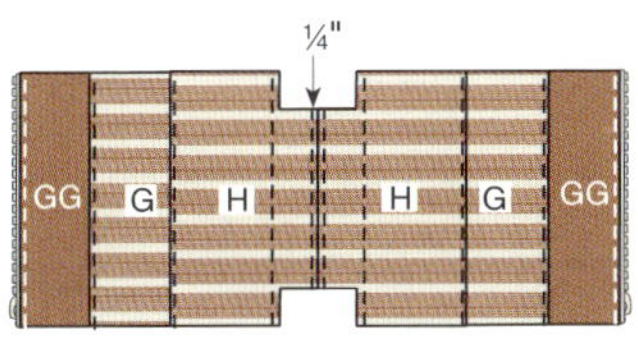

Figure 10

16. Lay the stitched panel with right side up; pin the I strap in place, aligning it 4½" from each side and matching seams on strap with bottom seam of the bag and pinning just to the top edge of the G panel. ***Note:*** *If seams are too heavy to sew over, realign seams with one side of the strip 1" above bottom seam and the other side 1" below the bottom seam as shown in Figure 11.* Stitch the I strap in place, starting and ending at the top of the G panels.

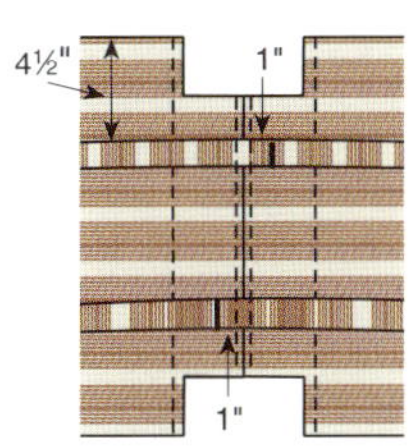

Figure 11

If using a striped fabric, cutting the straps so the fabric stripes are perpendicular to the stripes of the bag creates an interesting effect as can be seen in the photo above. This photo shows how the straps are stitched on and what the bag looks like when you are ready to stitch the panels together.

17. Close the zipper; sew a bar tack at the end of the zipper as shown in Figure 12.

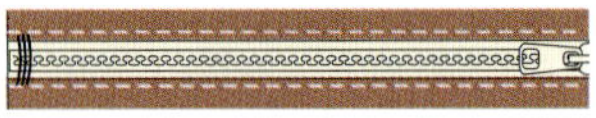

Figure 12

18. Leaving the zipper open enough to later turn the bag, join the panels at sides, matching seams and cutout corner edges as shown in Figure 13; press seams open. ***Note:*** *Do not stitch the edges of the cutout corners.*

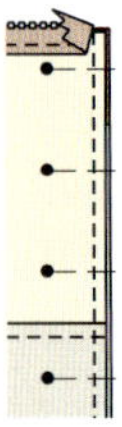

Figure 13

19. Fold zipper tape back at an angle at the zipper opening end; stitch on topstitching line as shown in Figure 14.

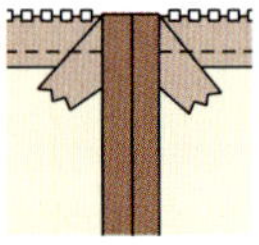

Figure 14

20. With right sides together, align side seam with bottom seam on one corner and stitch across the bottom/side seam as shown in Figure 15 to make a square bottom corner; repeat on the other corner of the bag. Turn bag right side out.

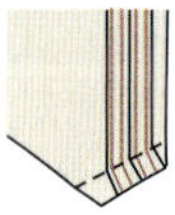

Figure 15

21. Push GG inside of G; topstitch ⅛" from the top of G, stitching across the straps as shown in Figure 16.

Figure 16

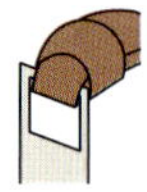

Figure 17

22. Fold the 6" strip of ⅜"-wide grosgrain ribbon in half; push folded edge through the zipper tab, forming a loop. Pull ends of ribbon through the loop as shown in Figure 17 to finish. ■

Extender Tote
Placement Diagram
Approximately 17¾" x 12½" x 5¼"

GUIDE
ON REVERSE SIDE.
VILLAGE
HILL

Handy Wallet

Keep your credit cards, money and other important documents inside this fabric wallet.

PROJECT NOTES

If you have already cut the pieces for the wallet as part of the set, proceed to Assembly Instructions.

PROJECT SPECIFICATIONS

Wallet Size: 7¾" x 11¾" open and 7¾" x 4" closed (includes binding)

MATERIALS

- ¼ yard 42"-wide non-quilted coordinating fabric with body
- ⅓ yard 42"-wide double-sided quilted fabric

TOOLS & SUPPLIES

- All-purpose thread to match fabric
- 2 (7") cream closed-bottom zippers
- 1½" length 5⅜"-wide hook-and-loop tape
- 25" length ⅞"-wide cream grosgrain ribbon
- Zipper foot
- Basic sewing tools and supplies

Cutting

Note: *Refer to Figure 1 for placement for cutting double-sided quilted fabric pieces.*

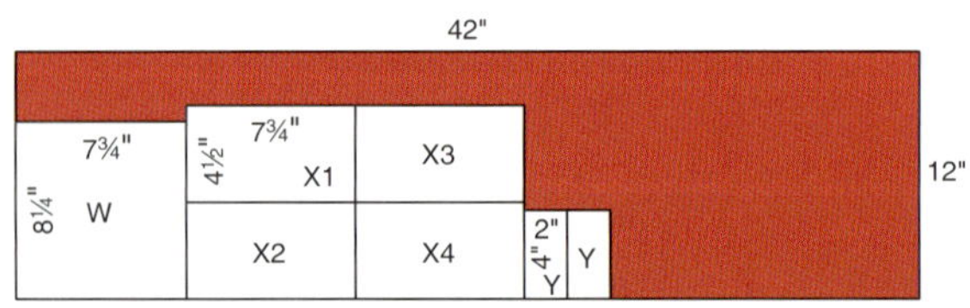

Figure 1

1. Cut one 7¾" x 8¼" W rectangle double-sided quilted fabric for top outside.

2. Cut four 7¾" x 4½" X rectangles double-sided quilted fabric and label X1, X2, X3 and X4 for pockets.

3. Cut two 2" x 4" Y rectangles double-sided quilted fabric for strap.

4. Cut three 7¾" x 4½" WIP rectangles coordinating fabric for inside pockets.

Assembly Instructions

Note: *Use a ⅜" seam allowance throughout unless otherwise noted.*

1. Using a quarter coin, round the corners of the top edge of each Y piece as shown in Figure 2.

Figure 2

2. Using a zigzag stitch, center and stitch the hook tape ¾" from top rounded edge on the right side of one Y piece as shown in Figure 3.

Figure 3

3. With right sides of Y pieces together, stitch ¼" from edges, from one side of the bottom to the other side as shown in Figure 4; clip curved edges. Turn right side out; press flat.

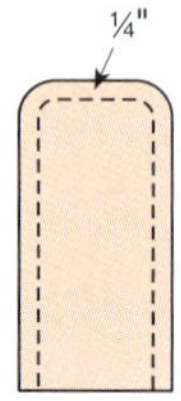

Figure 4

HOUSE OF WHITE BIRCHES, BERNE, INDIANA 46711 DRGNETWORK.COM

MB0328
SEC K
DRG
Dynamic Resource Group
PUBLISHING
Business
CHASE
macy's

4. Topstitch ¼" from edge to keep seams in place as shown in Figure 5; serge or zigzag across the bottom raw edges and set aside.

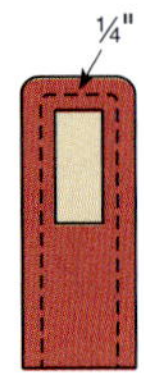

Figure 5

5. Referring to Figure 6, fold and press each WIP pocket in half along the long side; serge or zigzag long raw edge on two of the three pieces.

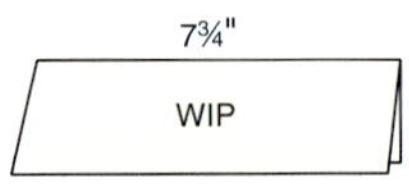

Figure 6

6. Fold and press serged edge under on serged line; stitch close to serged edge as shown in Figure 7.

Figure 7

7. Position one of the finished WIP pieces with the fold at the top, 1½" up from the bottom on the right side of the X1 piece; stitch in place close to the bottom of the WIP piece as shown in Figure 8.

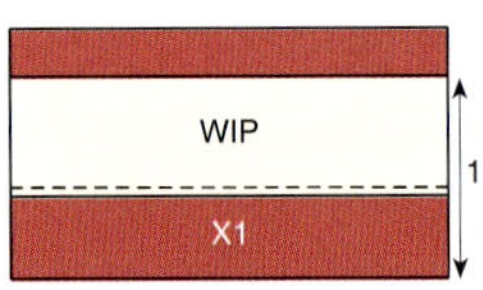

Figure 8

8. Position a second finished WIP piece with fold at the top, ⅞" up from the bottom on the right side of the X1 piece; stitch in place as shown in Figure 9.

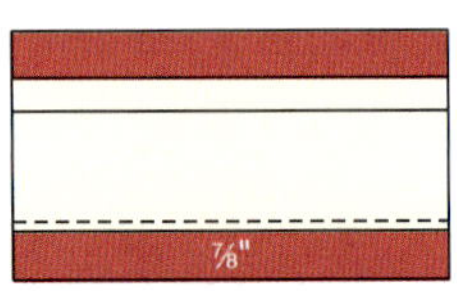

Figure 9

9. Referring to Figure 10, align the raw edge of the third WIP piece with the bottom raw edge of the X1 piece; stitch down the center of the three pockets. Serge or zigzag around the edges of the panel.

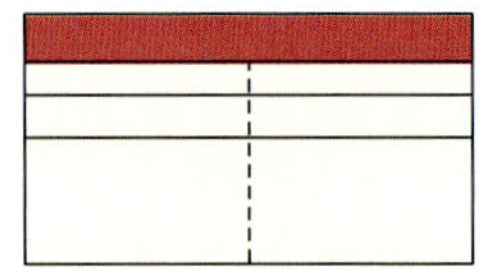

Figure 10

10. Fold under ¼" at the top and bottom of the panel; press and stitch close to only the top serged edge as shown in Figure 11; set aside.

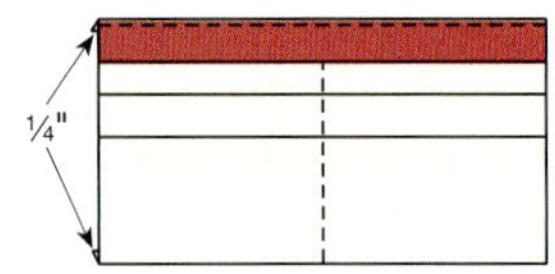

Figure 11

11. Serge or zigzag all edges of the remaining X pieces and the W piece.

12. Cut the remaining loop tape to 1". Using a zigzag stitch, center and stitch the loop tape 1¼" from the top right side edge of W as shown in Figure 12.

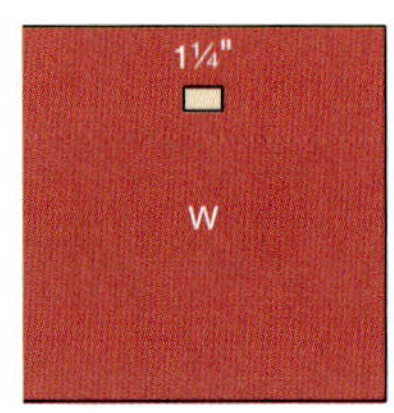

Figure 12

13. Press under ¼" to the wrong side at the top edges of the W and X2 pieces; mark in ⅜" from side edges on each piece. Lay pressed edges alongside the zipper teeth. Using the zipper foot, stitch close to folded edges of the W and X2 pieces, angling zipper tape back at ends of zipper teeth as shown in Figure 13. Stitch a second line ⅛" from the first line to hold zipper tape in place.

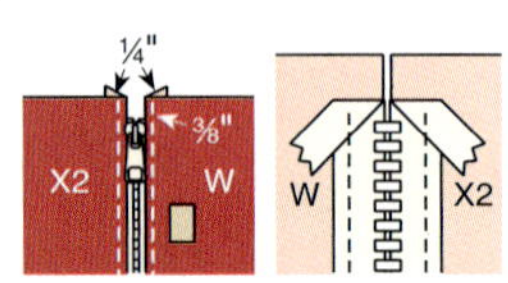

Figure 13

14. Referring to Figure 14, align side edges of W-X2 pieces; stitch at top of serger or zigzag stitching at the bottom of the X2 piece.

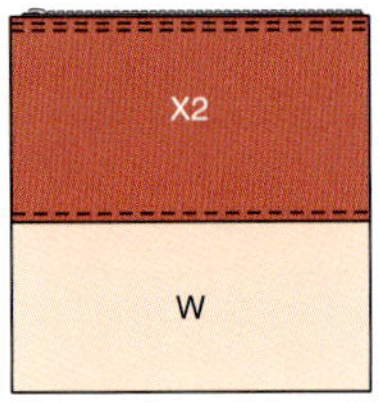

Figure 14

15. Press under ½" on one long edge of the X3 piece as shown in Figure 15; mark in ⅜" from side edges on the folded edge of the X3 piece and the bottom edge of the X1-WIP panel. Lay the bottom of the panel and the top of the X3 piece next to zipper teeth; stitch close to folded edges. Stitch a second line ⅛" from the first line on the X3 piece only. Cut off excess zipper tape.

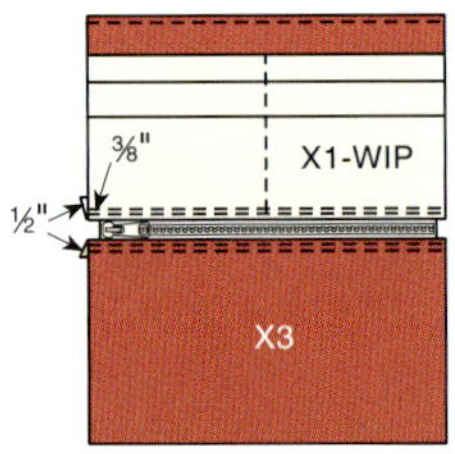

Figure 15

16. Center and baste-stitch the Y strap to the bottom of the front side of W as shown in Figure 16; align one long edge of the X4 piece right sides together with the Y-strap edge of W. Stitch ¼" from serged or zigzagged edges; press seam toward W.

Figure 16

17. Referring to Figure 17, align the X4 edge of the W-X4 panel right sides together with the X3 edge of the X3-X1 panel; stitch ¼" from edge. Press seams toward the X3 piece.

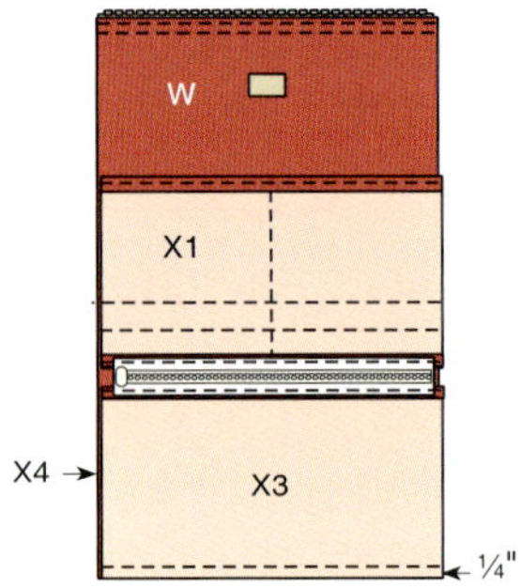

Figure 17

18. Fold the X3-X1 panel up; topstitch the seam allowance in place on the X3 side ¼" from seam line. Align side edges of both panels. Align zipper at bottom of X1-WIP panel with seam on W-X4 panel; machine-stitch on the X1-WIP panel ⅛" above first row of stitching at top of zipper as shown in Figure 18. Using the zipper foot, machine-baste side edges by serging or zigzag stitching, again referring to Figure 18.

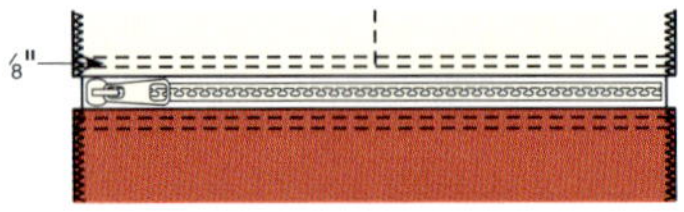

Figure 18

These photos, A and B, show the two sides of the panel before it is folded to create the many pockets and compartments that make this such a versatile purse.

19. Cut the grosgrain ribbon into two 12" lengths. With wallet laying open and inside facing up, align grosgrain ribbon with ½" extending above, below and to the side of the edges as shown in Figure 19. Using a long basting stitch, sew over the previous stitching.

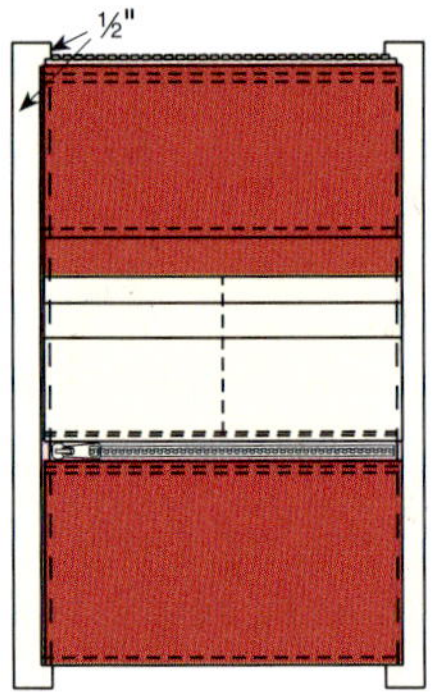

Figure 19

20. Fold ribbon over edges, enclosing previous stitching; fold ribbon ends in, covering the raw side edges. Topstitch ⅜" from wallet edge; remove basting stitches.

21. Fold wallet in thirds and fasten with strap to close. ■

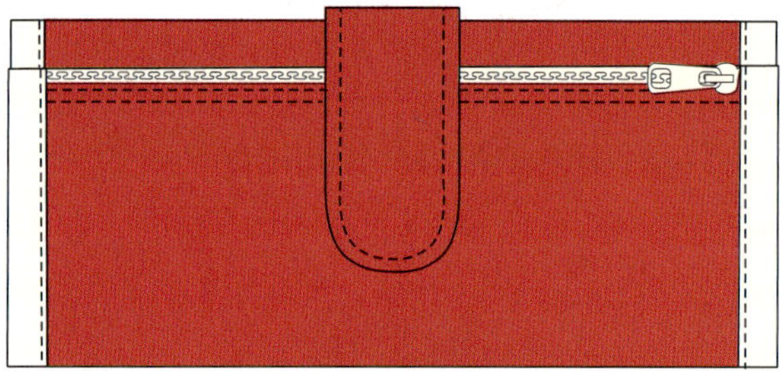

Handy Wallet
Placement Diagram
7¾" x 11¾" open
7¾" x 4" closed
(includes binding)

This photo shows the inside of the wallet with all its pockets and compartments before the grosgrain ribbon is added.

The outside of the wallet is fastened with hook-and-loop tape.

Mini Pocket Purse

Keep your change, keys and other smaller items organized in this little purse.

PROJECT NOTES

If you have already cut the pieces for this purse as part of the set, proceed to Assembly Instructions.

PROJECT SPECIFICATIONS

Purse Size: 7¾" x 4¼" x 1"

MATERIALS

- ¼ yard 42"-wide double-sided quilted fabric

SUPPLIES & TOOLS

- All-purpose thread to match fabric
- 7" cream closed-bottom sport zipper
- 6" length ⅜"-wide cream grosgrain ribbon for zipper pull
- Zipper foot
- Basic sewing tools and supplies

Cutting

1. Cut two 8½" x 5½" Q pieces quilted fabric.

2. Cut two 8½" x 5" QQ pocket pieces quilted fabric.

Assembly Instructions

***Note:** Use a ⅜" seam allowance throughout unless otherwise noted.*

1. Serge or zigzag across the 8½" edges of each QQ pocket piece.

2. Fold under a ½" hem on the top edge of each QQ pocket piece; press. Stitch close to serged or zigzagged edge.

3. Pin a hemmed QQ piece to the wrong side of each Q piece, matching bottom and side edges as shown in Figure 1; serge or zigzag-stitch side and bottom edges to hold.

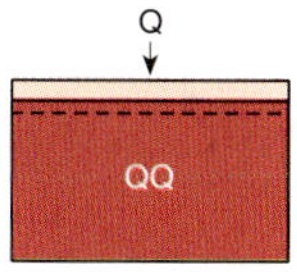

Figure 1

4. Mark the center and stitch from the top of the QQ pockets to the bottom edge to create two openings, again referring to Figure 2.

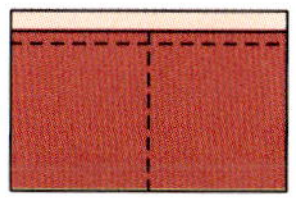

Figure 2

5. Mark in ¾" from side edges at the top of each Q-QQ panel; open zipper and lay face down on the right side of one panel even with top edge, placing the open end of the zipper at the ¾" mark. Using the zipper foot, stitch a ⅜" seam between the ¾" marks to attach zipper tape.

6. Fold zipper tape to the inside and topstitch ¼" from top edge of panel; repeat on the other side of the zipper on the other panel.

7. Open zipper; with right sides of panels together, stitch sides and bottom from the top of one side to the top of the other referring to Figure 3; press seams open.

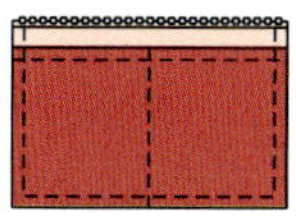

Figure 3

8. Fold zipper tape back on an angle at the zipper open end; stitch in place on the topstitching line as shown in Figure 4.

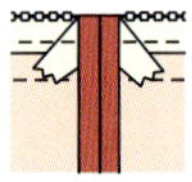

Figure 4

9. With right sides together, align side seam with bottom seam on one end and stitch ½" on both sides of the bottom/side seam as shown in Figure 5 to make square bottom corners; repeat on the other end of the purse. Turn right side out to finish.

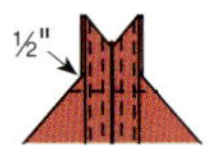

Figure 5

Figure 6

10. Fold the 6" strip of ⅜"-wide grosgrain ribbon in half to make a 3" double strip; push folded edge through the zipper tab, forming a loop. Pull ends of ribbon through loop as shown in Figure 6; cut ends diagonally. ■

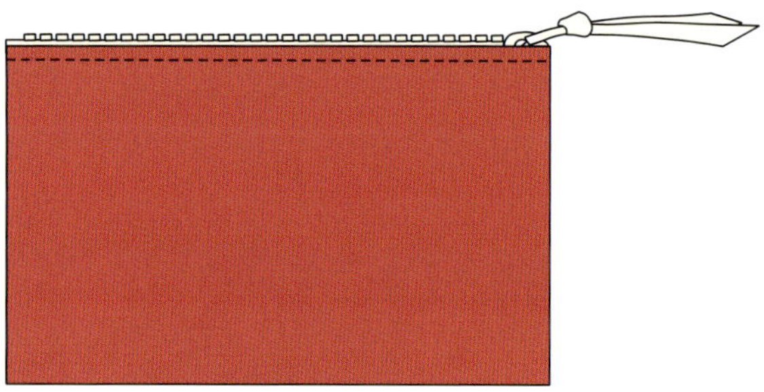

Mini Pocket Purse
Placement Diagram
7¾" x 4¼" x 1"

The two inside pockets on each side of this purse make it handy to use for storing those miscellaneous items that get lost in the bottom of a large purse.

The Weekender

When you need a bag to hold clothes for just a couple of days, this large zippered bag is perfect.

PROJECT NOTES

If you have already cut the pieces for The Weekender as part of the set, proceed to Assembly Instructions.

PROJECT SPECIFICATIONS

Bag Size: 18¾" x 16" x 6¼"

MATERIALS

- 1⅝ yards 42"-wide double-sided quilted fabric

SUPPLIES & TOOLS

- All-purpose thread to match fabric
- 2 (26") cream separating sport zippers
- 2 (6") lengths ⅜"-wide cream grosgrain ribbon for zipper pull
- Zipper foot
- Basic sewing tools and supplies

Cutting

Note: *Refer to Figure 1 for placement for cutting all pieces.*

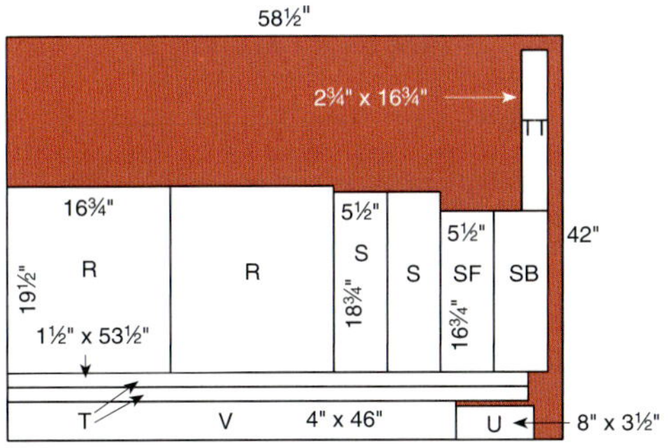

Figure 1

1. Cut two 19½" x 16¾" R rectangles for the body of the bag.

2. Cut two 5½" x 18¾" S rectangles for side panels.

3. Cut two 5½" x 16¾" strips for front and back side panels; label one strip SF and one SB.

4. Cut two 1½" x 53½" T zipper strips.

5. Cut one 2¾" x 16¾" TT back zipper strip.

6. Cut one 3½" x 8" U strip for handle.

7. Cut one 4" x 46" optional V strip for strap.

Assembly Instructions

Note: *Use a ⅜" seam allowance throughout unless otherwise noted.*

1. Serge or zigzag ends of U handle and V optional strap. Fold and press ⅜" of U handle to the wrong side on one long side and ½" on the other long side. Fold with fabric wrong sides together, matching pressed edges. Stitch ⅛" from open edge and ⅛" from folded edge as shown in Figure 2. Repeat with the optional V strap; set aside.

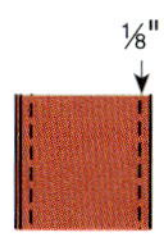

Figure 2

2. Serge or zigzag all edges of each T piece.

3. Open zipper; fold zipper tape end back at an angle toward the right side of the zipper as shown in Figure 3. Starting at the center of one T strip, position zipper face down on the right side of the T zipper strip, again referring to Figure 3. ***Note:*** *The edge of the zipper tape should be even with the serged or zigzagged edge of T and will extend ⅝" beyond the end of the T piece.* Stitch in place ⅜" from serged edges, stitching to the end of the T piece.

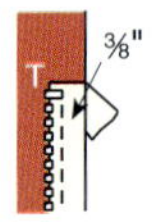

Figure 3

4. Fold zipper tape toward inside of strip and topstitch ¼" in from top fabric edge as shown in Figure 4; repeat with other zipper on the remaining end of the T strip. Repeat with remaining zipper halves on the remaining T strip.

Figure 4

5. Close zippers and sew bar tacks at the ends to keep them from separating as shown in Figure 5.

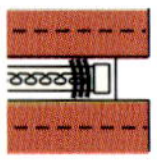

Figure 5

6. Serge or zigzag all edges of the TT piece. Place the T zipper strip right sides together with the TT strip. Stitch a ½" seam to join T/TT together, making a tube as shown in Figure 6. Press seams toward T zipper strips. Topstitch ¼" inside the T piece to hold seams in place, again referring to Figure 6.

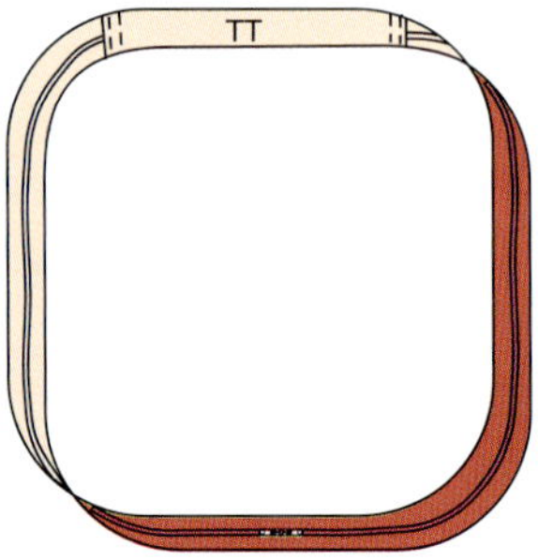

Figure 6

7. Serge or zigzag all edges of each S, SF and SB piece. Fold SF in half across the width and mark with a pin. Referring to Figure 7, place the stitched end of U 3" from the center and 2⅞" above the bottom of the SF piece; stitch across end on stitched line.

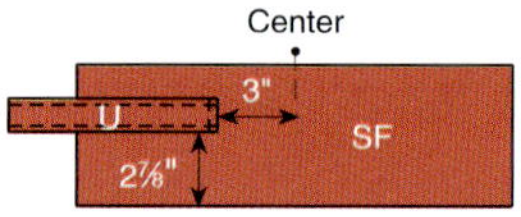

Figure 7

8. Fold the U handle piece back over itself; stitch again ¼" from the folded edge as shown in Figure 8; repeat at the other end of the U handle.

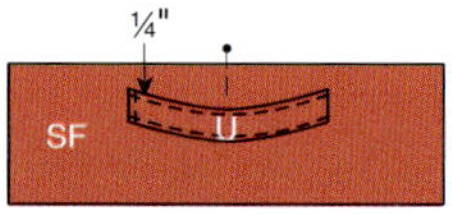

Figure 8

9. Machine-baste one end of the V optional strap 2¾" from the bottom of the SF piece as shown in Figure 9.

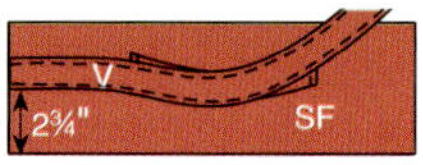

Figure 9

10. Position one S piece over the V strap; stitch together. Press seam toward S piece and topstitch ¼" inside S piece to hold seam allowance in place as shown in Figure 10; repeat with other end of strap.

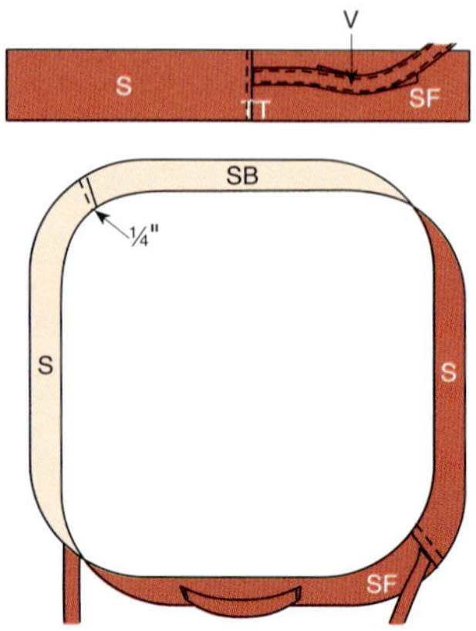

Figure 10

Notice how the T-TT zipper panel fits with the other pieces.

11. Join the SB piece to the unattached ends of the S pieces, making a tube, again referring to Figure 10; press seams toward S piece and topstitch ¼" inside S pieces.

12. Referring to Figure 11, fold the T-TT panel in half, aligning seams; mark folds at the top and bottom with pins. Fold in half again, lining up pins, again marking folds at the top and bottom with pins. Repeat process with S-SF-SB panel.

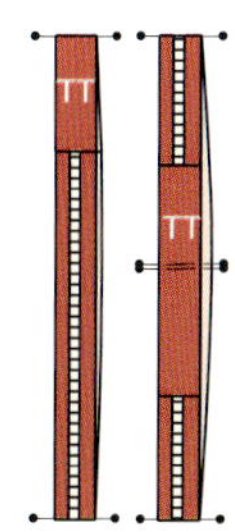

Figure 11

13. Referring to Figure 12, join the top of the S-SF-SB panel to the bottom of the T-TT panel with front sides of fabric together. ***Note:*** *The center of the T zipper piece should be centered on the*

SF panel, but the seams in the SB and TT pieces do not align. Press seam toward S-SF-SB panel; topstitch ¼" inside panel to hold seams together.

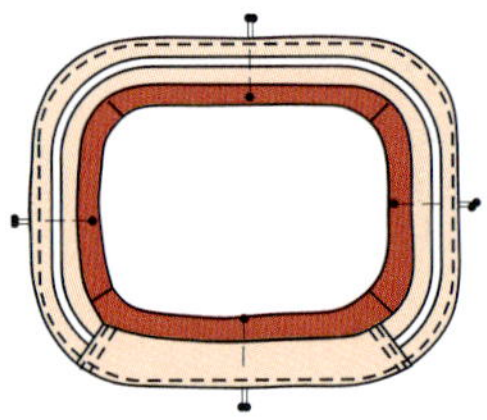

Figure 12

14. Prepare a template for the round corner pattern; place on each corner of the R pieces and trim to round corners. Serge or zigzag all edges of each R piece. Referring to Figure 13, fold each R piece in half vertically and horizontally and mark folds with pins to mark quarters.

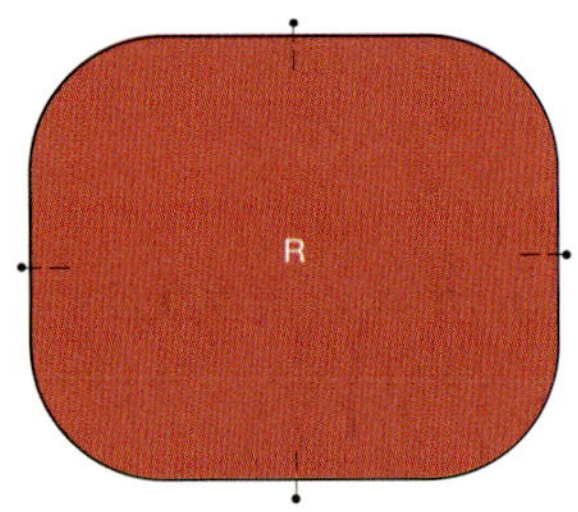

Figure 13

15. Referring to Figure 14, with right sides together, match pins on R bottom piece with pins on the bottom of the S-SF-SB panel. ***Note:*** *The center of the zipper opening on T/TT panel aligns with the center on the long side of the bottom R piece, and the seams align at the corners of the bottom R piece.*

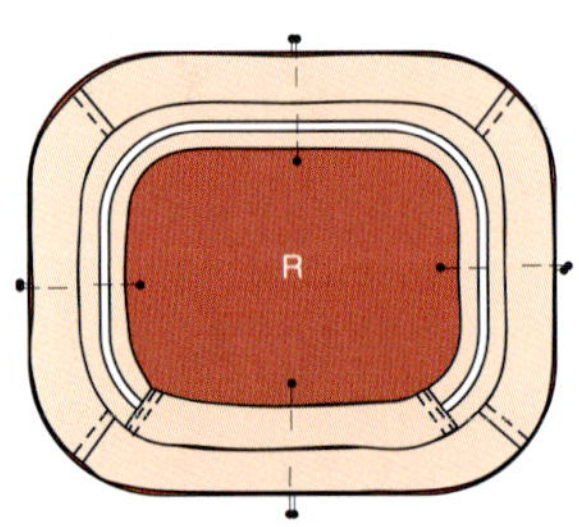

Figure 14

16. Stitch S-SF-SB panel and R bottom piece together; press seam toward the panel. Topstitch on the panel ¼" from seam line to hold seam allowance in place.

17. Unzip the zipper and repeat steps 15 and 16 with the R top piece, pinning the right side of R to the right side of the T-TT panel. ***Note:*** *The seams on the T-TT panel do not align with the corners of the top R piece.*

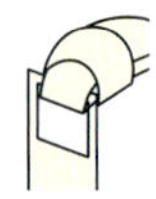

Figure 15

18. Fold the 6" strip of ⅜"-wide grosgrain ribbon in half to make a 3" double strip; push folded edge through the zipper tab, forming a loop. Pull ends of ribbon through the loop as shown in Figure 15 to finish. ■

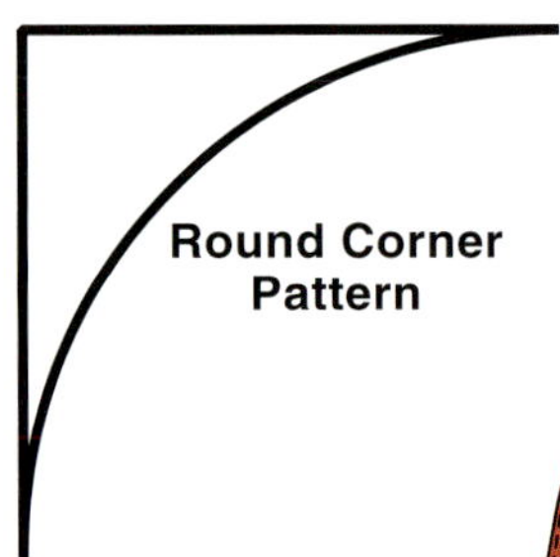

Round Corner Pattern

The Weekender
Placement Diagram
18¾" x 16" x 6¼"

With both a handle and a shoulder strap, this bag is ready for any occasion.

Meet the Designer

Jerry Shaw

Jerry Shaw designs and makes bags, totes and purses for her business, *Purses by Jerry*. In this, her second book, she shares designs and instructions for bags and purses of various sizes.

Although upholstery fabric is the fabric of choice in her business, she also enjoys using quilted fabric. She finds it easier to sew than upholstery fabric, even though the latter is more durable and produces a very different look.

Jerry has been married to her husband, Ray, for 45 years. They have four beautiful daughters, two wonderful sons-in-law and four adorable grandchildren. Since her first publication, their oldest grandson is driving; their only granddaughter was in a horrible accident but is back to her passion of playing soccer; their second grandson is learning to play the piano; and their youngest grandson has been diagnosed with autism, which has added a new dimension to all their lives.

Jerry enjoyed the challenges of this book and still loves showing her purses and totes at local craft shows and area groups. One of these days you may find Jerry's bags for sale on eBay. So look for Ms.Jerry Shaw there.

E-mail: Customer_Service@DRGNETWORK.COM

HOUSE of WHITE BIRCHES
PUBLISHERS SINCE 1947

Quilted Travel Bags is published by DRG, 306 East Parr Road, Berne, IN 46711, telephone (260) 589-4000. Printed in USA.

RETAIL STORES: If you would like to carry this pattern book or any other DRG publications, call the Wholesale Department at Annie's Attic to set up a direct account: (903) 636-4303. Also, request a complete listing of publications available from DRG.

ISBN: 978-1-59217-187-3
1 2 3 4 5 6 7 8 9

STAFF

Editors: Jeanne Stauffer, Sandra L. Hatch
Managing Editor: Dianne Schmidt
Technical Artist: Connie Rand
Copy Supervisor: Michelle Beck
Copy Editors: Sue Harvey, Nicki Lehman, Judy Weatherford
Graphic Arts Supervisor: Ronda Bechinski
Graphic Artists: Debby Keel, Edith Teegarden
Art Director: Brad Snow
Assistant Art Director: Nick Pierce
Photography Supervisor: Tammy Christian
Photography: Don Clark, Matthew Owen
Photo Stylists: Tammy M. Smith, Tammy Steiner